GET ON THE BULL

Developing Attitudes and Behaviors
for Successful Leadership

DALLIN COOPER

Get on the Bull:
Developing Attitudes and Behaviors
for Successful Leadership
by Dallin Cooper

Copyright © 2022 by Dallin Cooper

ISBN (paperback) 978-1-0880-4211-3
ISBN (hardcover) 978-1-0880-4218-2
Also available as a Kindle e-book

Editing by Shannon Dunn, Editing Insights
Cover and interior design by DTPerfect.com
Interior image design by Dallin Cooper

For quantity sales or other inquiries, please contact the author at
www.DallinCooper.com

CONTENTS

PART ONE

PART TWO

FOREWORD

When he gets on a bull, the cowboy's goal is an 8-second qualified ride.

Working for 8-seconds on top of a bull may seem simple, but just like everyone who aims to succeed at anything, there are many layers to reaching that desired goal.

As the CEO of the Professional Rodeo Cowboys Association (PRCA), and former ProRodeo cowboy, seeing the grit and determination of a bull rider to succeed against all odds is something I relish witnessing. My ties and what I have learned through being part of the rodeo lifestyle have been a catalyst to the leadership role I am in today at the PRCA.

Through the mindset of a bull rider, Dallin Cooper takes readers on a motivational journey to better their own lives. Dallin has definite ties to bull riding. He grew up listening to stories from his father and former bull rider Steve Cooper. He was fascinated by his father's lifestyle and the daily trials and tribulations on the trail to succeed in rodeo.

Dallin explores all the elements of what a bull rider goes through to achieve success and how it relates to the lives of everyone. Cooper creatively conveys his points by sharing the traits and actions that make up the bull rider attitude. The readers can relate to overcoming obstacles and adversity just like bull riders do every time they climb aboard a 1,500-pound bull who wants to throw them off into the arena dirt.

As Dallin writes, plenty of people—not just bull riders—face overwhelming daily challenges. Some people overcome those challenges. Others don't.

Dallin accepted the challenge to write this book. Through parallels of a bull rider, he conveys his message in a simple, creative, and motivational manner. So, "Get on the Bull" with him, apply what you learn to your everyday life, and enjoy the ride.

— Tom Glause
CEO, Professional Rodeo Cowboys Association

INTRODUCTION

Bull riders are masters of moments. On the back of a bull, eight seconds can feel like a lifetime. For perspective, the 2021 PRCA World Champion Bull Rider, Sage Kimzey, successfully rode 88 bulls at competitions. That amounts to approximately twelve minutes of bull riding throughout the entire year.

Twelve minutes.

Hundreds of hours in training, both physical and mental, went into making sure that he could instinctively make the right decisions in those split-second moments when he was on the bull—a year of work and effort defined by twelve minutes.

Leadership is defined by moments. It isn't a title or position. Leadership is a lifestyle. All the seemingly insignificant moments work together to define our habits and character. The attitudes and behaviors that we develop in our day-to-day lives determine how we act in pivotal moments. The attributes of effective leadership need to be so ingrained in us that they become second nature.

Becoming a good leader can be difficult. Many fulfilling and transformative things in life are. One of the reasons I loved listening to my dad's bull riding stories growing up was because they were stories of him and his buddies overcoming obstacles and doing difficult things.

But bull riders aren't the only ones who confront the seemingly impossible. Plenty of other people face overwhelming challenges every day. Those challenges may not have hooves or horns, but they're no less dangerous. Some people overcome those challenges. Others don't. Some people talk about starting a business. Others go out and create one. Some dream of their potential. Others take steps to reach it. Some wait to be led. Others lead.

Some choose to walk away and take the easy way out. Others get on the bull.

HOW TO USE THIS BOOK

Many of us hear stories, read books, or listen to speeches that make us want to be better. Motivating and inspiring, they leave us thinking, "This time, I'm really going to change."

But all too often, we don't.

We're inspired by the motivational feelings and get excited to do things differently. Still, ingrained habits and behaviors are difficult to change. We get swept up in the hustle and bustle of daily life and revert to our default attitudes.

That's where Implementation Intentions come in.

Change requires a specific plan. So, at the end of each section in this book, you'll find suggestions of ways to develop the attitude or behavior that was just covered. You'll also find an example Implementation Intention and some spaces to write your own.

Very simply, an Implementation Intention is a specific plan that helps you reach your goals. For example, a goal might be, "I'm going to be more active." A great goal, but it's vague. An Implementation Intention for that goal would be, "If I see an elevator, I'm going to look for stairs. If I find stairs, I will take them." Implementation Intentions are usually some sort of "If…then" statement that conditions your brain to react a certain way when you're in a specific situation. It helps you pre-choose the desired behavior so it's easier to do when the opportunity arises. Perhaps even more importantly, it helps you recognize the opportunity in the first place. Effectively using Implementation Intentions drastically increases the odds of reaching your goals and sticking to a positive behavior long enough for it to become a habit.

This book is supposed to be fun. The principles of effective leadership aren't anything new. But I've always learned best from stories and metaphors that were memorable and impactful. Hopefully, the unique stories in this book make you think about these classic principles in a new way.

But this book is designed to be more than just a fun read. It's meant to transform your life. That's why in addition to stories and analogies, each section will have suggestions for how to develop the attribute as well as example Implementation Intentions and room to write your own. There are also lined pages at the back of the book to write your thoughts, goals, or plans. Feel free to write in the margins, highlight favorite sections, and ask yourself questions. If you want to develop the attitudes and behaviors of effective leaders found in this book, deliberately act on what you read. Use the suggestions provided and create thoughtful, personalized Implementation Intentions.

PART ONE

CHAPTER ONE

THE BULL RIDER ATTITUDE

"RIDING IS REALLY A MENTAL GAME."

GARY LEFFEW

It shouldn't surprise you that bull riders have a unique attitude and mindset. It takes a special kind of person to look
at 1,600-2,000 pounds of hulking, furious muscle and say,
"I need to strap myself to that and see whether it can throw
me off." But the bull rider attitude goes far beyond just doing
something that most people think is crazy. It's present in all
aspects of their lives. It's how they see themselves and those
around them. It's how they handle setbacks and mistakes—as
well as their triumphs and successes. Bull Riding isn't just a
sport. It's a lifestyle.

Leadership must be part of your lifestyle. You can't have
an "ethical leader" mode at work that you turn off when you
leave the office. Like a bull rider, your attitude at home, work,

and everywhere you go will determine your success. And I'm not just talking about your financial success, but also success in your relationships, hobbies, and anything else you value. Success in anything begins with your attitude.

There are four elements of a bull rider attitude that you can start applying in your life immediately to become a better leader, a better friend, and a better person.

CHAPTER TWO

DETERMINED OPTIMISM

"OPTIMISM—IS NOT JUST A MINDSET, IT IS BEHAVIOR."

LARRY ELDER

Getting on a bull takes determination and a whole lotta courage. But a willingness to get on isn't the most impressive part of bull riding. No. The most impressive part is that the riders get on *knowing* that the odds are against them! The average rate of successful rides amongst professional bull riders is around 30%. So, these guys go out there knowing that there's a 70% chance that they're gonna get thrown. But each time, they sincerely believe that *this* time, they'll succeed. *This* time, they're going to do it.

Because if you don't believe that you can, you won't.

If you half-heartedly get on the bull's back while saying, "I guess I'll give it a shot, and maybe he'll let me ride him," You're toast. It's over. That bull will dump you faster than a middle school crush.

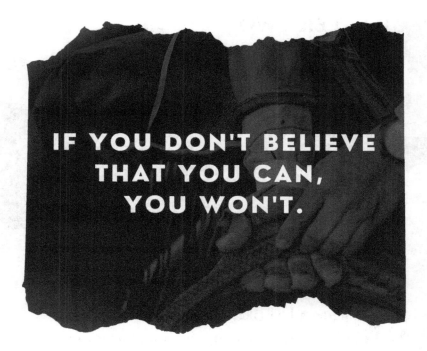

IF YOU DON'T BELIEVE
THAT YOU CAN,
YOU WON'T.

And it isn't that bull riders are in denial. Every single one of them has fallen off before. They know they'll get thrown again, but they go after each opportunity with enthusiasm and belief. That relentless optimism is critical to their success, because whether you win or lose is often completely determined by your thoughts. Gary Leffew, Pro Rodeo Hall of Famer and perhaps the most successful bull riding coach *ever*, is well known for saying, "Riding is really a mental game." At his school, he teaches riders to meditate often, vividly imagining themselves successfully staying on the toughest of bulls. He's fond of saying, "Whatever you vividly imagine, ardently desire, sincerely believe in, and enthusiastically act upon, must inevitably come to pass." While that principle has its limits, it highlights a fundamental truth. Gary's students learn to imagine success so clearly and so frequently that they come to sincerely believe they can ride anything. And once they believe they can ride the toughest bulls, they usually do.

And Gary's technique isn't just effective for bull riding. Mental rehearsal, sometimes simply called visualization, is used in most sports with great success. A well-known study by sports psychologist Dr. Judd Biasiotto showed the power of mentally rehearsing success. He had three groups of students that played basketball shoot free throws and recorded their results. Then he had one group practice shooting free throws for 30 minutes every day for 30 days. One group never touched a basketball but mentally visualized successfully making free throws for 30 minutes every day for 30 days. And one group didn't practice at all. The group that didn't practice at all showed no improvement (big surprise!). But the group that practiced daily and the group that only visualized practicing both improved at nearly the exact same rate. Their performance improved simply by vividly and accurately believing they could succeed.

Effective leaders need that same relentless optimism. But a leader's job is more difficult than simply learning to believe they can accomplish their goals. They also need to believe in the people they lead and then get those people to believe in *their* goals. Let's look at two different ways a leader could introduce their team to a wonderful but challenging opportunity.

Negative Leader: "Well guys, this is going to be difficult, and statistically speaking, we'll probably fail. But we should probably try anyway, and maybe it'll work out."

Bull Rider Leader: "We have an amazing opportunity, and it's going to push us to do our very best. It will be hard, but I know that we can absolutely knock it out of the park."

Which leader would you rather follow? I know I'd rather follow the determined and optimistic leader. Not only would it be way more fun, but most studies agree that the optimistic leader is more likely to succeed. Specifically, a 2021 study by the American Psychological Association looked at several different impacts of optimism. They found that those with consistent optimism were more likely to reach their goals and experienced less stress while doing so. The APA even put the final nail in the coffin of pessimism with this study. One of the only widely accepted drawbacks of optimism is the belief that getting your hopes up just makes failure or disappointment even more unpleasant. But this study indicated the opposite! Those who were optimistic but failed anyway *still* reported lower levels of distress and disappointment than those with a less positive outlook. Determined optimism only served to fuel their resilience and belief that they would overcome the setback.

The "optimism" part of determined optimism is more than just blind hope that it will all work out. It requires situational awareness (the accurate knowledge of the position you're in and its likely potential outcomes) and making the conscious choice to move forward, believing that you can achieve the desired result. The bull rider is aware that getting thrown is a possibility, but *chooses* to believe they can succeed. Without knowing your situation, there's no possibility of choosing a realistic but hopeful outcome. Intentional, determined optimism cannot co-exist with ignorance.

The "determined" half of determined optimism indicates that this isn't a passive attitude. You can't just get on the bull with no training, no preparation, and no knowledge then expect to be successful. An essential element of determined optimism is doing everything within your power to accomplish your goals. When challenges and obstacles obstruct the path, determined optimists *choose* to believe that those challenges can be overcome and that they will reach their intended goal, even if it takes years.

So, when the stakes are high and the challenges are intimidating, follow the path of a bull rider leader and move forward with determined optimism.

DEVELOPING DETERMINED OPTIMISM

Whether from nature or nurture, determined optimism comes easier to some people than others, but anyone can develop this attitude. To view yourself and the world with hope and positivity is a choice. When you choose to alter your thought processes, you can literally rewire your brain to think more optimistically. And these brain changes can happen more quickly than you'd think! One study found that significant neurological changes occurred within two months of consciously changing thought patterns.

The first step is to make the choice and commit to yourself that you're going to practice determined optimism, even when the obstacles seem overwhelming. Then, consider some of the following ideas:

- Spend time with positive people. Take a careful inventory of how you feel around your friends, family, and acquaintances. Pay attention to how they talk. Make an effort to spend more time with those who are encouraging, uplifting, and positive. Try to minimize time spent with those who are discouraging, negative, and complaintive.

- Consume uplifting media. There is so much positive and uplifting content in the world! Unfortunately, there is also plenty of less uplifting (and even just plain negative) media. Social media and news in particular, tend to be more negatively framed because negative news usually generates more revenue. This is because our brains are wired neurologically to focus on the negative rather than the positive. It takes conscious effort to train it otherwise. Try to limit your exposure to negatively skewed media and sources that rely on "outrage" for money.

- Practice mental reframing. When you notice yourself becoming frustrated, discouraged, or pessimistic, actively counter those thoughts with positive "silver linings." It's cliché, but it works. Acknowledge the negative while *actively choosing* to also notice the positive. You can do this in your head, verbally to a confidant, or in a written format like a journal.

IMPLEMENTATION INTENTIONS

Remember to make an Implementation Intention that is specific and frequent. The point is to create a new habit by tying a positive behavior to something you do often. I've included an example that you can use, but I encourage you to use the space provided to create an Implementation Intention that is tailored to your own goals.

- Every morning when I get to work, I will envision one thing that I have scheduled today going well (in detail).

- _____
  _____

- _____
  _____

CHAPTER THREE

HUMILITY

"A HUMBLE PERSON IS MORE CONCERNED ABOUT WHAT IS RIGHT THAN ABOUT BEING RIGHT, ABOUT ACTING ON GOOD IDEAS THAN HAVING THE IDEAS...ABOUT RECOGNIZING CONTRIBUTION THAN BEING RECOGNIZED FOR MAKING IT."

STEPHEN M.R. COVEY

Determined optimism will help you overcome a lot of challenges, but at times you will still fail. You *will* get bucked off the bull. The best—the very best—bull riders still fall off more than half the time.

And what do they do when they fall off?

Well, there are two answers to that question, and they happen in a very specific order.

First, they get up and get out of there! Just because they're no longer on the bull's back doesn't mean they're safe. There's still nearly a full ton of angry bovine rampaging across the arena. So the first priority is to get the heck out of the ring without any major injuries!

Second, they start preparing for the next time by looking at what they did wrong, what they did right, and determining how they can improve.

This perfectly echoes how an effective leader should handle mistakes or crises.

First, do the necessary damage control. Stabilize the situation so there won't be further damage. Then deal with the immediate aftermath with honesty, humility, and pragmatism.

Second, learn from what went wrong, what went right, and work to improve.

Notice a few things that are distinctly absent: excuses, blame, and deceit. That's because a bull rider must know how to humbly accept failure and handle mistakes with grace. They don't say things like "The bull cheated!" or "It wasn't fair!" or "The gatemen messed me up!" Instead, they dust themselves off, learn from the past, and move on. Because what else is there to do? Some days you win, and some days the bull does.

An effective leader knows they'll make mistakes. But they acknowledge their mistakes, learn from them, and try to do better. They know that blaming others or trying to make excuses only degrades trust and stifles their ability to learn. This level of accountability requires humility. We can't worry about looking good or saving face. When we stop worrying about making ourselves look good, we eliminate the need for blame, excuses, coverups, and deceit. It also empowers us by freeing up all the mental energy we *would* have used on worrying, which we can then use to lift others!

Warren Buffett, who I think we can all agree could be labeled "successful," gives a great example of humbly accepting responsibility in his 2015 letter to shareholders. He had this to say when explaining how the year went:

> "Some of this sector's businesses, measured by earnings on unleveraged net tangible assets, enjoy terrific economics, producing profits that run from 25% after-tax to far more than 100%. Others generate good returns in the area of 12% to 20%.
>
> A few, however—these are serious mistakes I made in my job of capital allocation—have very poor returns. In most of these cases, I was wrong in my evaluation of the economic dynamics of the company or the industry in which it operates, and we are now paying the price for my misjudgments. At other times, I stumbled in evaluating either the fidelity or the ability of incumbent managers or ones I later appointed. I will commit more errors; you can count on that. If we luck out, they will occur at our smaller operations."

At that time, Warren Buffett had a net worth of $67 billion. People have labeled him "The Oracle of Omaha," and many have called him the greatest investor of all time. With that much success and recognition, it would be easy for pride to get the best of him. But Warren has internalized an attitude of humility. So, instead of blaming his subpar investments on a volatile market or on poor managers (which he does mention, but without laying the blame at their feet), he takes responsibility for his misjudgments and poor evaluations. What makes this so much more impressive is that he did it in a situation where he likely didn't need to. He could have gotten away with blaming others and focusing on the successes instead. But he was humble enough to admit he made some bad calls along with the good ones. And obviously, it's worked out for him. In the last six years, that $67 billion has increased to over $103 billion.

Learning to humbly deal with failure is significantly more important than avoiding mistakes. In fact, handling mistakes with grace is actually more effective for building trust than *not* making mistakes in the first place. Study after study has shown that when leaders openly and transparently admit their mistakes instead of hiding them, those they lead trust them more and will reciprocate that honesty. Not only that, but a boss' willingness to admit their mistakes has been proven to be one of the best ways to positively impact their employees' job satisfaction and desire to stay in their jobs. Whether employees, customers, friends, or family, people won't be shocked to find out you make mistakes. They already know that. What they want to know is how you handle it. Instead of trying to convince those you lead that you don't make mistakes, let them see your mistakes, and then let them see you make them right.

WHAT'S AN EXCUSE?

Eliminating excuses is a hallmark of humility. But what exactly counts as an excuse? Is there a way to explain your behavior without "making excuses?" The answer to that question is a resounding yes! Not only is it possible, but at times it is crucial. Excuses hold leaders (and everyone else) back by degrading trust and taking away valuable opportunities to learn. But **reasons** can help us learn while simultaneously building trust. Once again, we can look at Warren Buffett's letter to shareholders for an excellent example of giving *reasons* instead of *excuses*.

"In most of these cases, I was wrong in my evaluation of the economic dynamics of the company or the industry in which it operates, and we are now paying the price for my misjudgments. At other times, I stumbled in evaluating either the fidelity or the ability of incumbent managers or ones I later appointed."

Notice these key phrases: "...**I was wrong** in my evaluation..." and "...**I stumbled** in evaluating..." See how he keeps the responsibility for any mistakes squarely on himself? The main characteristic of an excuse is to avoid responsibility, blame, or consequences. They are used to minimize the severity of the mistake or to make yourself look better. They are used to hide.

Reasons are used to *explain*. They provide context and information so that similar situations can be avoided in the future. They are used to learn and provide clarity. Reasons also help initiate conversations about problems that lead to creative solutions.

Recognizing your intent when discussing mistakes is the most effective way to identify whether you're providing reasons or making excuses. You can ask yourself, "Am I phrasing it this way to stay out of trouble or make myself look better?" If the answer is yes, then it's probably an excuse. Ironically, eliminating excuses from your life will actually affect how people see you in a positive way. Your authentic humility will make a more significant impact than shallow excuses ever could when you stop trying to impress people with false perfection.

Excuses vs Reasons

Intent may be the biggest difference between reasons and excuses, but wording still plays a major role. Here are some examples of very similar reasons and excuses. Take note of the difference between "blaming language" and "explaining language."

Excuses	Reasons
Sorry, I'm late. Traffic was crazy.	Sorry, I'm late. I forgot to plan for holiday traffic.
They made me mad.	I lost control of my temper.
We met the deadline, but the shipping company has delayed your order.	When we created our timeline, we failed to account for the holiday shipping rush.

HUMILITY IS NOT WEAKNESS

Humility is not self-deprecation. It is not being a pushover. It is not assuming you are wrong or doubting your abilities. Many people try to appear "modest" by self-handicapping. They downplay their talents and abilities, even those they truly excel at. This is not humility. It's actually the opposite. Self-handicapping is used as a method of protecting our pride and self-esteem. If you seek challenges well below your ability, you'll be more likely to excel. If nobody expects much from you, then you can't disappoint them. If you don't claim to be good at anything, you can never fall short. If you don't really care or try your hardest, then it won't hurt as bad if you fail.

Exaggerating weaknesses and downplaying your strengths is not the path to humility. In fact, the only way to achieve true humility is to acknowledge and embrace your strengths along with your weaknesses. A humble leader recognizes their value as well as everyone else's. They can be confident in their abilities without bragging, exaggerating, or blustering. They can acknowledge their weaknesses without turning to excuses or self-pity. Perhaps more than anything else, the ability to be humble is what truly sets great leaders apart from simply good leaders.

SHARE EXPERIENCES

My sister, Shay, is a basketball coach. She's coached at middle and high schools in various locations over the years, but her experience coaching in one particular small town taught me a powerful lesson. And when I say small town, I mean a *really* small town. The last census lists the total population at 842. So the pool of basketball talent was limited, and their program didn't typically have much success. In fact, they hadn't won a single game in several years. But that didn't deter Shay. She coached those kids with every expectation that they could become great. When they scrimmaged in practice, she had each team run a lap for every avoidable mistake. For example, if the offense gave up a turnover, they ran a lap. If the defense allowed an offensive rebound, they ran a lap. Since their numbers were so few, Shay sometimes played to fill out one of the teams. And when her team made a mistake, she was right there running along with them. And if she made a mistake, they would all run with her.

At the end of each year, Shay had a fiercely loyal basketball team who would go to the ends of the earth for her. That loyalty was a result of her behaviors. She didn't put herself above them. She wasn't exempt from the rules. She shared in their triumphs, mistakes, struggles, and successes.

There is power in sharing your team's experiences. Too many leaders insulate themselves from the challenges and triumphs of those they lead. It takes humility to willingly submit yourself to trials and discomfort, but it helps you better understand those around you while building loyalty with everyone involved.

This principle is so powerful that it's largely responsible for the outcome of the Revolutionary War. The winter encampment at Valley Forge is often described as the turning point of the war and the birthplace of the American Army. It's also described as a frigid, miserable experience where everybody was ill, hungry, and destitute. The army was on the brink of collapse. They had no supplies, and many of the men didn't even have shoes. The Continental Congress was considering replacing George Washington as general. But over the course of that winter, everything changed. Though some deserted and far too many died, the trials of that winter forged the remaining men into the American Army–a formidable fighting force united by their cause and in their loyalty to General Washington.

What caused a half-starved rabble of farmers and workers to undergo such a major transformation in such terrible circumstances? Simple: Their loyalty to a man who stayed when he didn't have to. He was struggling right along with them, eating their tooth-breaking hardtack and sleeping on the frozen New England dirt. And even more impressively, Martha Washington was as well! She came to tend the sick and offer as much comfort as she could to anyone she came across. Despite having a luxurious, warm estate at Mount Vernon with butlers, maids, and food aplenty, the Washingtons stayed with the army and shared in their suffering. That decision led to victory in the war and eventually to George Washington being elected the first President of the United States.

While both Shay and George Washington show the value of being present with those you lead, that isn't always possible. If you manage large teams, you may be leading hundreds of people stretched across different countries. There's no way to physically be everywhere all the time. In these circumstances, make an effort to see people face-to-face (yes, video conferencing counts) and work with them directly, even if it's only occasionally. More importantly, share in their successes and challenges, even from afar. Have a video call with a group to congratulate them after they make a breakthrough or reach a goal. Offer expertise or resources when they're struggling. Be as present as possible.

HOW TO DEVELOP HUMILITY

Acknowledging mistakes, accepting failures with grace, and being present with your team are only a few aspects of humility. Truly humble leaders demonstrate humility in everything they do. It isn't something that can be faked. But just like the act of smiling can make you feel happier, behaving humbly can help you *become* more humble. Consider incorporating some of the following behaviors into your life to help you develop humility:

- Form an accurate self-image. Most people either overestimate their ability and ignore their faults or overestimate their faults and ignore their strengths. Few people have a truly accurate view of themselves. Working with those close to you to create an accurate personal image will help you in more ways than just developing humility. When you understand your strengths and weaknesses as they truly are, it is easier to ask for help, offer help where you can, and handle mistakes gracefully. Forming an accurate self-image is a massive undertaking and would require an entirely separate book to address in detail. You may want to start by writing what you think your strengths, weaknesses, biases, cognitive blind spots, and talents are. Then check your list against those who know you best to help correct where your perception may be distorted.

- Assume you *aren't* the smartest person in the room. Regardless of your own brilliance, there is always plenty to learn from others. Actively seeking new information in a sincere way not only makes you better, it shows a humble willingness to learn. And it earns the respect of those you learn from.

- Admit what you don't know. The whole point of having teams that work together is that everyone on the team has different strengths and can cover each other's weaknesses. It's your job as a leader to bring all those strengths together. It's important to recognize when you may not have the knowledge necessary to solve a problem or make a decision. You'll be more effective if you utilize your team's expertise, and you'll be more trustworthy because of it. It's okay to ask for help, explanations, or opinions.

- Serve. You'll find more details on serving later in this book. Service deflates ego by reminding you that titles, positions, money, and accolades don't make you better than anyone else. Helping others and expecting nothing in return will keep you grounded.

- Express gratitude. Gratitude and humility have a cyclical relationship. Gratitude makes you more humble. Humility makes you more grateful. The next section is all about gratitude, so read on for more!

IMPLEMENTATION INTENTIONS

- When I make a mistake, I will tell someone about it so I can actively take responsibility and avoid excuses.

- _____
_____

- _____
_____

CHAPTER FOUR

GRATITUDE

> "AS WE EXPRESS OUR GRATITUDE, WE
> MUST NEVER FORGET THAT THE HIGHEST
> APPRECIATION IS NOT TO UTTER
> WORDS, BUT TO LIVE BY THEM."
>
> JOHN F. KENNEDY

B ull riders are the superstars of the rodeo world. They get the most hype, the coolest headlines, and the biggest jackpots. Bull riding is usually the last event in a rodeo, acting as the grand finale. You would think that this environment would cause bull riders to be pretty full of themselves. But if you ask a bull rider who the most important people in the rodeo are, you'll probably get one of two answers. One of the most common answers you'll get is, "The bullfighters."

If you aren't familiar with rodeo, when you hear "bullfighter," you might think of red capes and shouts of "Olé!"

But we aren't talking about matadors. The bullfighters we're talking about often get confused with rodeo clowns. That's because, for many years, bullfighters and rodeo clowns were one and the same. To this day, many bullfighters will still wear silly makeup just to honor the tradition. However, in most modern rodeos, they serve two separate functions. The rodeo clown (or barrelman) provides entertainment by telling jokes, sassing the announcer, and doing physical comedy, including (more or less safely) hanging out in a barrel during the bull riding.

Bullfighters provide a significantly more serious service. You may mix them up with the clown at first glance because of their colorful, loose, and somewhat raggedy-looking clothing, but bullfighting is no laughing matter. Their job is to distract the enraged bull after a ride so the rider can escape to safety. So yeah, if you think the bull riders are hardcore, take a second to think about the guy who steps between them and the bull and says, "You run, I'll hold him off!"

Cody Webster, one of the best bullfighters in the world, described his job by saying:

> "It's kind of like we're the Secret Service men for the… bull riders. We're going to be there to protect them at all costs, and that can be as simple as just distracting a bull but sometimes having to put our body on the line and take a shot for a guy."

They may not make the headlines, but any bull rider knows that you give the bullfighter all the credit, respect and praise in the world. When asked about bullfighters, four-time national qualifying bull rider Jeff Askey said:

> "You can't count the amount of times in a year that they've saved your butt. There's so much that can happen right there, and them taking that bull away from you just for a few seconds…is the difference in your season being a month long or making it all year."

Like all bull riders, Jeff understands that his success, safety and life rest in the bullfighter's hands. And that is exactly how you should feel about those you lead. If a great leader accomplishes anything amazing, it is because hardworking individuals are making it happen. And they don't get the praise and recognition they deserve from the general public, but they better get it from their leader.

Former Secretary of State Colin Powell said the following when it came to recognizing those you lead:

> "There is no end to the good you can do if you don't care who gets the credit. The 'credit others' mindset is fundamental for impactful leadership. If something goes well and people notice, they already know you're the leader and played an important part in the success. You don't need to remind them. Instead, take every opportunity to highlight the work of those who aren't in the spotlight. People respect leaders who make them feel valued, and that value is much more important than an outsider's opinion."

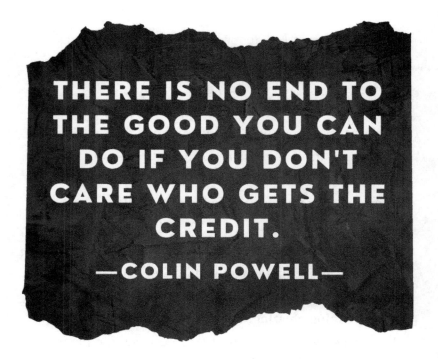

THERE IS NO END TO
THE GOOD YOU CAN
DO IF YOU DON'T
CARE WHO GETS THE
CREDIT.

—COLIN POWELL—

The other (and actually most common) answer I've received when asking bull riders who should get all the respect and credit in the rodeo is one that might surprise you.

The bull.

What? The bull? Why should the rider be grateful for the bull? Isn't the bull who the bull rider is competing against? Well...actually, he isn't. The bull is who the bull rider is competing *with*. To win a bull riding competition, a rider needs to have the highest total score, with each ride being worth a maximum of 100 points. The bull rider is judged based on how well they ride. Are they in control? Are they balanced? Are they making the right adjustments to stay on the bull? A bull rider who does everything perfectly can earn a maximum of 50 out of 100 points. The other 50 points come from the bull.

The bulls are scored based on how fast, aggressive, and difficult they are to ride. So the bull isn't actually an enemy. It's a partner. And the best riders really do see it that way. Gary Leffew said, "The goal is to dance with [the bull]...When you're dancing, you become one with the person you're with...You're so mentally in tune with them, you go there together—and it's a euphoric experience." It isn't uncommon to see cowboys finding the bull they've drawn and praying with them, because it isn't enough to just stay on the bull. You need the bull to be amazing as well. To win, the cowboy NEEDS the bull to buck its heart out. It needs to be a challenge. You'll never win a rodeo by staying on a gentle bull.

Successful leaders know that growth comes from overcoming adversity. People don't become great by looking at challenges and saying, "Eh, that looks hard. I'll do something easier." Truly great leaders are the ones who welcome challenges as an opportunity to learn, grow, and accomplish amazing things.

In 2017, Heather Monahan was fired from her job as Chief Revenue Officer of a large radio group. She spent 14 years, the vast majority of her career, working for this company and climbing the corporate ladder to the C-Suite, only to be terminated shortly after reaching her goal. It was devastating. But instead of letting this set her back, she used it as an opportunity. A year later, she published her first bestselling book. Then came a podcast and another bestseller. Four years after she was fired, she was named one of the top 50 keynote speakers in the world. Heather's message has a consistent theme of gratitude that she didn't end up where she originally wanted and that obstacles were thrown in her path. Those challenges helped her become the person who would eventually achieve her dreams.

The challenge isn't your enemy. It's your partner. What's the point of a company or an organization without a problem that needs solving? It's about as useful as a rider without a bull.

Like a bull rider, a good leader needs gratitude for their team and the challenges they work to overcome.

HOW TO DEVELOP GRATITUDE

Cultivating gratitude is primarily about awareness. Your exercises in humility will help with this. Instead of fixating on all the good they do themselves, a grateful leader identifies and praises the good that others do. Consider some of the following ways to increase your awareness of and gratitude for those around you.

- Thank people frequently and specifically. Move beyond just "Thank you" to specifying *why* you're thankful. Set a daily goal for expressing gratitude X number of times.

- Trade negative self-talk for positive expressions of gratitude. Change "Sorry for bothering you" to "Thank you for your time." Switch out "Sorry I'm late" for "Thank you for your patience."

- Keep a gratitude journal. Each day, set aside time to write down a few things or people you are grateful for, being as specific and in-depth as possible. Make an effort to avoid repetition, and come up with new things to be grateful for each day. You may begin with the example pages found in the back of this book.

IMPLEMENTATION INTENTIONS

- When I say "I'm sorry," I will change the sentence to be a "Thank you," even if it involves awkwardly stopping mid-sentence and starting over.

- _____
  _____

- _____
  _____

CHAPTER FIVE

PERSPECTIVE

"WE NEVER SEE THE FULL PICTURE.
WE CANNOT KNOW A PERSON'S LIFE
AND CHALLENGES AT A GLIMPSE. WE
NEVER HEAR THE FULL STORY. WE
CANNOT GRASP A PERSON'S VIEWPOINT
THROUGH MERE WORDS. WE NEVER FEEL
THE FULL PAIN. WE CANNOT PERCEIVE
A PERSON'S HEART AND MIND IN A
CONVERSATION."

RICHELLE E. GOODRICH

An effective leader needs to understand those they lead. Unfortunately, years of psychological research has taught us that we're *really* bad at understanding other people. We say things like, "Put yourself in their position." But one of the reasons that doesn't work is that when you put yourself in that position, **you are still yourself.** You don't think like they do, you don't view the world the same way, you don't have the same experiences, and so on. Even right now, you're experiencing this book differently than anyone else who has ever read it. You may be inferring, making connections, coming up with real-world applications, and learning things that I could never have foreseen when writing it! Because we're all complicated beings with a lifetime of influences that shape how we interpret the world around us. And that complexity makes it incredibly difficult to understand each other by simply putting ourselves in another's shoes.

In fact, one study found that it doesn't help at all. Participants were given a limited profile of information on a person and then asked to actively imagine their perspective based on that small profile. The researchers referred to this exercise as "perspective-taking." After completing the perspective-taking exercise, the participants answered questions about the person whose profile they had been given. In the end, the researchers found that participants who engaged in perspective-taking performed **the same as, if not worse than,** those who didn't make an effort to understand the subject at all. The only thing that changed with the exercise was that the perspective-takers were more confident that their wrong answers were correct. That's right, regardless of race, gender, or social position, when we try to imagine what other people are feeling, we tend to get it wrong while simultaneously patting ourselves on the back and saying, "Man, I'm so good at this empathy thing!"

So how do we understand those we lead if perspective-taking actually makes it worse?

Luckily, that same study provides the answer. The researchers found that it's far more productive to engage in what they called "perspective-*getting.*" Perspective-getting can take several forms, but it always involves gathering new information instead of making assumptions based on past information and incomplete information. It turns out that the simplest method of accurately understanding someone's perspective is also the most obvious method.

Ask them.

That's right. When you want to know how someone feels about something, you can ask them.

When my wife and I got married, we were both still full-time college students, and I was desperately trying to create a successful business on the side. Due to some previous family financial trauma that she'd gone through as a teenager, she was a little worried about the instability of entrepreneurship. But I was determined to show her that we could "make it!" Not only did I want my business to succeed, but I also wanted to make all her wildest dreams come true. And I wasn't necessarily patient about it. Without realizing it, I flipped into work-myself-to-death mode. Every spare second I had was spent trying to make the business grow and succeed. On her end, she rapidly developed skills critical to our success and significantly accelerated our progress. And so, we worked away in our tiny one-room basement apartment until one Saturday she

41

voiced a frustration that I didn't even know she had but had clearly been building for a while.

"Can we just do something fun for once today?" she suddenly blurted out.

Wait...what? That is not the question you want to hear from your new wife.

"What do you mean?" I asked.

"We used to do so many fun things! We would go to the mountains and hike, we would go rock climbing, we would do...things! I feel like ever since we came back from our honeymoon the only thing we've done is work. I know money is tight, but can't we spare a few dollars and a few hours to just go have some fun? I'm glad we're seeing some success, but I'm going to go crazy if working is all we ever do!"

And that was the moment that I felt like an idiot. Because I realized she was right. My intentions were good, but I was so focused on making her big dreams come true so she could be "happy" that I never thought to ask her what would actually make her happy *right now*. On the other side of the coin, she had seen my fervent devotion to our work and assumed (incorrectly) that I didn't have the need or desire for recreation. She knew I was stressed about our money situation and didn't want to make me more stressed by suggesting we spend some of our precious time and dollars on something so "frivolous" as recreation. In the end, both of us had ended up spending months making incorrect assumptions about each other's feelings, and those assumptions had only made us more miserable. Once we started *using our words* and communicating about our perspectives, the whole matter was cleared up within a day.

And with that newfound understanding and clear perspective, we were both able to change the way we talked and behaved and became a whole lot happier. My dad had a similar experience bull riding that helps illustrate how gaining perspective changes how we treat those around us.

A STORY BY STEVE COOPER

To practice riding, a lot of bull riders will build a practice bull of some type. I built a contraption using a barrel and a counterweight. One person would get on the barrel, and someone else would operate a lever to spin them around and whip them up and down. One of my buddies, who was not a bull rider, would sometimes watch us practice, and now and then he would hop on the practice barrel. We'd always tell him, "Now David, you really gotta get a holt of that rope." He'd say, "I'm holding the rope," and we'd say, "No, David. You gotta get a *holt*! That doesn't just mean to hold on to the rope. It means you hold on with *everything*—your hand, your legs, your feet, and your soul better be holding on to that bull." And he just didn't seem to get it. He'd still just always give us a hard time, saying, "Holt isn't even a real word."

Eventually, the day came that David decided he wanted to try riding an actual bull, not just the practice barrel. So we found him a nice little easy bull that we were pretty sure wouldn't break him. We got him all geared up and settled in the chute, and we said, "Now David, before we open this chute, you bear down and *really* get a holt of that bull rope." The chute went flying open and a few seconds later, David went flying too! He stumbled to his feet, pulled himself out of the ring, looked at me and said, "Now I know what you mean when you say, 'Get a holt.' That is a completely different experience that I was totally unprepared for."

44

Unfortunately, we can't always gain a clear perspective in four seconds as David did.

Why?

Because people are complicated. A million different factors affect how each person perceives the world. Where and how we were raised, the people we've been around, our experiences, and more all weave a unique tapestry that creates our perspective. And even if you get on and ride the exact same bull as someone else, you're going to have a completely different ride. Not only are you a different person with different experiences, desires, goals, and ideas, but the bull itself is never going to buck exactly the same way twice.

However, just because we can never perfectly understand each other's perspectives doesn't mean we shouldn't try. Making an effort can help both you and the people you lead simply because they'll see you doing just that: **making an effort.** Just remember that you won't always get it right. But it's about the principle. A leader who cares enough to ask, to learn, to try and understand is a leader who will not only be more effective but will earn the loyalty of those they lead.

GOOD VS. BAD JUDGMENT

When I was a teenager, I had an experience that will probably be familiar to you. Like most teenagers, I was excited to get my driver's license and enjoy the freedom that came with it (especially since I grew up in rural Wyoming, ten miles away from the nearest town). Also, like most teenagers (and many other people for that matter), I sometimes found myself frustrated by other drivers. *Why are they driving so slowly? Why are they driving so fast? Why are they so reckless? Why don't you look to see if I'm going to hit you before cutting me off?* I wasn't a road-rage monster, but I sometimes got frustrated. One morning on the way to school, I was cruising down the highway and had to slam on my brakes to avoid a herd of deer crossing the road. The driver behind me swerved into the other lane, blasted his horn, and threw me the finger, all while completely missing the deer herd just a few feet away in the darkness.

He drove away thinking I was an idiot, I drove away thinking *he* was an idiot, and we both made great examples of the Fundamental Attribution Error (FAE). The Fundamental Attribution Error is a cognitive bias that causes people to judge themselves by their intentions while judging other people by their behavior. When I cut someone off in traffic, I still consider myself a good driver who just made a mistake. When someone cuts me off, it's because they're an idiot who doesn't know how to drive.

However, my experience with the deer made me start to question this tendency. After all, I don't know what's going on in someone else's life. Perhaps I should offer them the same benefit of the doubt that I would like to be given.

As a leader, making judgments comes with the territory. For example, when you're hiring, it's literally your *job* to judge which candidates will be a good fit. You judge which people will be best in what roles. You make judgments when offering pro-motions or raises. Making accurate judgments about people's capabilities is crucial to leadership success. But you must be careful to eliminate personal bias and the pesky Fundamental Attribution Error.

These biases are often deeply ingrained, so recognizing and eliminating them is incredibly difficult. It takes a great deal of self-awareness. One habit that can help identify personal biases is to watch out for labels. Biases tend to become our mental short-cuts. They're ways for our brain to skip out on the hard work and just make quick assumptions based on past experiences.

Our brain is already hardwired to work this way, and much of the time, that's actually a good thing. Can you imagine hav-ing to calculate the pros and cons of every decision you ever have to make? Think about how many decisions you make be-fore you even get to work in the morning! What are you going to wear? Are you going to eat breakfast? If so, what will it be? What's the best way to get to the office? Luckily, our brains have a vast well of memories, previously created neural path-ways, and sensory information to draw upon that make these decisions so easy as to require little thought. You *are* going to eat breakfast because that's the habit you've established. It's go-ing to be a bagel because that's what you eat every morning. And you know your commute like the back of your hand, so that'll be no biggie. Presto—decisions made!

But while these mental shortcuts (broadly referred to as heuristics) are helpful in our menial, everyday decisions where the consequences are small, they tend to leave us with lazy and broad assumptions if we rely on them for bigger, more important judgments. If your feelings about a situation or person (including yourself) can be summarized in just a word or two, then those feelings are likely inaccurate. At the very least, it's a sign that you lack crucial information and context. Because, once again, people are incredibly complicated and nuanced. The FAE would have us label someone as lazy when the reality is likely much more intricate. Perhaps they're in a position that lacks performance incentives and they're also struggling with insomnia that leaves them exhausted during the day. They get their work finished but are by no means overachieving. Or the employee you think is slacking off with their long and frequent bathroom breaks actually has Crohn's Disease. Perhaps the co-worker who was "being a real jerk" was on edge because they just got off a phone call where they learned their brother had been diagnosed with cancer. And the list could go on and on.

You often won't be aware of these types of problems, and most of them aren't your problems to solve. And you definitely shouldn't try to unless directly asked for help, advice, or a specific service. When in doubt, you should always gravitate toward compassion. It's impossible to know the circumstances surrounding everyone's lives and behavior. And if you try to guess, you'll probably get it wrong. So when you find yourself in a position where you have to make judgments, just remember that all of these people **are people**. They aren't numbers, statistics, employees, candidates, or customers. **They are**

people. People with hopes, dreams, struggles, and challenges that are no more or less important than your own.

So while you can't hire every candidate, you can remember how nerve-wracking your first job interview was and how badly you hoped someone would just give you a chance. You can inform those you didn't select that the position was filled and offer feedback or help if they want it.

You can't give everyone the promotion, but you can consider how much it hurts to be passed over for one. And you can provide transparent reasoning for your decision, as well as bonuses and meaningful responsibility for those who were also qualified to be promoted but weren't.

In all your decisions, consider that you will be affecting the lives of countless people who all have trials and circumstances that you know nothing about. Make your decisions with compassion and understanding for those people.

Does that sound a little exhausting? Emotionally draining? Immensely time-consuming?

Good.

It should. Being a leader means that what you do will fundamentally alter other people's lives, for better or worse. So take a note from Spider-Man and remember that with great power comes great responsibility. The responsibility to care and to consider the perspectives outside your own when making those decisions.

You will have times where it is your duty as a leader to make a judgment call. But just because it's your duty to judge doesn't mean it's your duty to label. But remember, it's *always* your duty to care.

DON'T GET DESENSITIZED

Most leaders want to care. They want to consider other people's perspectives. They want to be a great leader. Odds are *you* are one of those leaders who want to be great! You wouldn't spend your valuable time reading this book if you didn't care.

But good intentions aside, every leader faces a common enemy that can destroy their ability to connect with those they lead, sometimes before they can even get started. That enemy is desensitization. Desensitization is what stops great leaders from caring, making good judgments, and remembering to gain perspective. So what do I mean by desensitization? Let me explain with an example.

In 1986, the Space Shuttle Challenger exploded, taking with it the lives of seven astronauts. The explosion was caused by exhaust gasses that leaked through a failing O-ring. In turn, the O-ring's failure was caused by the abnormally cold temperatures the morning of the launch. The rockets were rated for a minimum launch temperature of 39 degrees Fahrenheit. The morning of the launch, it was 24 degrees Fahrenheit. Officials delayed the launch in hopes that it would warm up and they could move forward. Despite warnings from engineers, the decision was made, and the shuttle was launched at 11:38 a.m. when it was still only 36 degrees. When presented in that light, the decision seems at best negligent, and at worst, absolutely psychotic.

But the Dispute Resolution Research Center at Northwestern University found a way to help people see this decision in a little bit of a different light. They created a case study that included the same risks, rewards, payoffs, and data (including the exact numbers) that were provided to NASA's decision-makers but framed it to be about deciding whether they should race a car instead of launch a rocket. The case study was designed to show how factors such as time, pressure, perceived risk, and ambiguous data can affect decision-making. When this dilemma was presented to 250 business management students, around 95% of them made the exact same decision as NASA. They decided the risks were worth it and moved forward.

When the students learned that this was actually a simulation of the Challenger launch, they were shocked, appalled, and indignant. And I would know because I was one of the students who did this case study in college. I'm ashamed to say that I made the same decision as the NASA team did. But, like many participants, I felt that I would have made a different decision if the stakes had been made more evident. I even voiced thoughts like, "If I knew that people could die if things went wrong, I would have made a different decision." But the case study facilitator quickly shut me down, explaining that engine failure in a high-speed race definitely runs a risk of death, although most of the data provided was financial. The decision-makers for NASA were also faced with significant financial and technical data that drew their attention away from things like safety. Like many other participants I talked to who have also done this same case study, its lesson has profoundly impacted my perspective. It showed how quickly we can get desensitized to actual people by numbers, data, or even just repetition.

Desensitization happens everywhere. You see it when competent, dedicated doctors and nurses treat patients impatiently. It may be the scariest day of the patient's life, but for the doctor, it's just Tuesday. You see it in a realtor who communicates poorly because they're closing on five houses in the next week, while the first-time homebuyer is freaking out because this is the biggest financial decision they've ever made. Whether you're a marketer, manager, mechanic, plumber, or accountant, *your* hum-drum day-to-day may be a **big deal** to someone else.

For the people at NASA, their desensitization cost not only millions of dollars but seven lives–a fact I'm sure they struggle to live with even to this day. It may not always feel that way, but desensitization can be just as catastrophic in your organization. If a bull rider gets desensitized and stops respecting the danger of the sport, they can get hurt or even killed. If you get desensitized and lose perspective as a leader, it can cost people their health, livelihood, relationships, and in more cases than you might think, their very lives.

Your actions have consequences. Your decisions have consequences. Don't let them become habitual and complacent. Don't allow yourself to get desensitized. A thoughtless decision can be a catastrophe, but a thoughtful one can be miraculous. **You** have an impact.

You wield more power than you believe. Maintain a healthy perspective, be deliberate, and strive to turn each of your everyday little decisions into someone else's miracle.

HOW TO DEVELOP PERSPECTIVE

As the study mentioned in this section notes, the best way to develop perspective is to recognize that your perspective isn't the only valid one. Then try to gather new information to expand your understanding. Some ways to practice "perspective-getting" include:

- Work on active listening. Ask clarifying questions to make sure you understand what you're being told and that you're interpreting it the correct way.

- Avoid assumptions. They're usually wrong and prevent perspective-getting behaviors.

- Understand your own perspective. Maslow's Hierarchy, The Bible, and airplane safety procedures all agree that you need to help yourself before you can safely help others. It's difficult to understand someone else's feelings and worldview if you don't even understand your own. Make an effort to identify your own thought patterns, biases, priorities, and cognitive blind spots.

- Travel. If it's within your means, try visiting places with different cultures than yours. Getting outside your bubble and seeing an entire world where the way **you** do things is weird is an excellent way of realizing the limits of your own perspective and bias.

IMPLEMENTATION INTENTIONS

- When I get frustrated with someone or criticize them, I will stop to ask myself what incorrect assumptions I might be making.

- _____
  _____

- _____
  _____

IT TAKES TIME

S hifts in attitude and thinking habits don't happen over-night. Just like bull riding, it takes practice. Harkening back to Gary Leffew's lesson that bull riding is a mental game, one of his strategies to improve was, "Riding bulls every day in [his] mind...experiencing what it was like to ride and win over and over again." Mastering your thoughts and attitude takes discipline, but more than that, it takes patience. It takes intentionally creating positive thought patterns over and over again. But as you implement the suggestions on developing each element of a bull rider attitude, you will see changes in how you think. And those changes will inevitably impact the way you behave for the better.

I had the opportunity to interview Seth Glause, a former professional bull rider and current rodeo coach. This principle of patient progression was a clear theme throughout our inter-view while he talked about his own bull riding career, as well as how he helps his students improve. His philosophy as a coach is to work on incremental growth instead of trying to be perfect overnight.

"We review film, look at what went right, and pick one thing to work on and move forward. Sometimes people get caught up in trying to fix the whole picture instead of making small adjustments that create a better result over time."

Seth learned the importance of that strategy from his own difficult experience. At the 2012 National Finals Rodeo, he battled through a broken nose in the second round and a dislocated shoulder in the fifth to eventually come out 2nd at the NFR and 3rd in the world rankings. 2012 had been a great year! But because of his injury, he missed most of the 2013 season, having surgery and recovering. In 2014 he came back with a vengeance! He was ready to surpass his 2012 performance and become the best in the world. And then he hurt his shoulder again. And again. The surgery he endured shortly after that made it clear that he was never going to competitively ride bulls again. Injury is inevitable in bull riding, but Seth was adamant that his attitude contributed to his frequent injuries. He described it by saying, "I was trying to win the world title on every single bull, instead of making it a culmination of a lot of good rides that build up over time. I was trying to force it. You have to just do your best with each opportunity instead of getting too focused on the big goal at the end."

Just like Seth, it's easy for us to get burned out by focusing too much on giant changes or massive tasks. We all have plenty to work on, but if you try to fix every inadequacy at once, you'll just get frustrated and not fix any at all. Instead, let your journey toward being a better leader be a culmination of good decisions that build up over time. You can't force it.

PART TWO

CHAPTER SIX

Bull Rider Behaviors

> "BUT WHEN YOU CHANGE YOUR ATTITUDE, YOU CHANGE YOUR BEHAVIOR. WHEN YOUR BEHAVIOR CHANGES, SO DO YOUR RESULTS."
>
> **WILL HURD**

Your changes in attitude will naturally change your behavior and make you a better leader. But can you also make conscious changes to your *behavior* to help change your *attitude*? It's a classic chicken-and-the-egg dilemma. Does your attitude dictate your actions, or do your actions change your attitude?

The answer? YES!

Mindset and behavior are intrinsically linked. As you change one, the other is affected. By actively working on both, your growth as a leader and well-rounded person can be significantly accelerated.

In one of my interviews with a bull rider who will remain anonymous, I heard a story about a man trying to impress a young woman. He told her he was a bull rider and a cowboy and went on and on about how tough and manly he was. But she'd met a lot of bull riders and cowboys, and there was something that didn't line up with his attitude. Obviously, nobody is perfect, but most of the bull riders she'd met had all the attitudes that you've just read about: they were humble, grateful, optimistic, and tenacious. This arrogant young man (who ended up being the epitome of a "wannabe tough guy") was none of those things, and you could tell. His behavior spoke volumes. A true rider doesn't need to tell you how tough they are. They don't need to try to impress you. Because even if they don't try, their attitude and behavior will naturally impress you anyway.

Margaret Thatcher once said, "Being powerful is like being a lady. If you have to tell people you are, you aren't."

We can apply that same principle to leadership. If you have to tell people that you're a great leader, you probably aren't one. Instead, great leaders show their quality through their behavior. The behaviors discussed in this section will help you act in a way that makes you a powerful leader, regardless of your title.

CHAPTER SEVEN

HONESTY

"YOU DON'T ALWAYS HAVE TO CHOP WITH THE SWORD OF TRUTH. YOU CAN POINT WITH IT TOO."

ANNE LAMOTT

I hope it isn't news to you that lying isn't super ethical and is terrible for building trust. Even though most of us would say that we know honesty is good, the average person still lies 11 times a week. Despite the many differences in people's upbringing, race, political affiliation, religion, etc., the fact that *lying is bad* is something that virtually everyone can agree on. So why do we all still do it?

There are really only two reasons people lie: selfishness or fear. We can all easily think of obvious, malicious, or direct lies. These are the lies that are usually motivated by greed or selfishness—the kinds of lies that "bad guys" tell in movies. As a bonus, they're often illegal, like lying to a customer about a return or refund policy just to make the sale. You know these lies are bad, and I know they're bad, and there's not a whole lot of gray area in there. But for those of us who aren't supervillains, most of those 11 lies a week are much more subtle. They're half-truths, misdirections, or intentionally withholding the truth. These are usually the lies that "good" people tell–people who consider themselves ethical. And the reason they worm their way into the lives of good people is because they're so easily justifiable.

HALF A TRUTH IS OFTEN A GREAT LIE.

—BENJAMIN FRANKLIN—

These lies usually have good intentions. We tell ourselves we lie to spare someone else discomfort, pain, or sorrow. Maybe we tell ourselves that we're protecting them or that you just want them to be happy. Those reasons are real and valid, but they aren't the *entire* reason. Deep down, we're also lying because we're afraid–afraid of what they'll think of us, afraid of having to clean up afterward or perhaps afraid of what the truth will do to the relationship. Here are some examples of common lies, our "good" reasons for them, and the full reasons we might tell them.

Lie	The "good" reason	The full reason
That design/ presentation looks great!	I don't want to make them uncomfortable or insecure.	I also don't want to deal with the discomfort or confrontation from offering negative feedback.
I'll be there in 5 minutes!	Maybe I can actually make it in 5 minutes!	Okay, so it may be a little closer to 10, but I don't want them to start without me!
That email must have gone to spam or something.	I don't want them to think that they aren't important.	I also don't want to look stupid and forgetful.
I'm fine.	I don't want to worry them with my problems.	I also don't want them to view me differently because of my problems.

Being honest can be scary and uncomfortable. But bull riders know that fear and discomfort are just part of the process. To get the prize money (and that sweet, coveted belt buckle) at the end of the rodeo, you have to face down your fear and hang on through your discomfort. Instead of using lies to try to avoid the fear and discomfort, which basically never works, we need to confront them and work through them. Many bull riders face a dilemma like this in the beginning of their careers. How they handle this challenge determines their future.

A STORY BY STEVE COOPER

I was probably about 14 years old, and it was only the second time I had ever ridden an actual full-sized bull. As it neared my turn, the rider two spots before me was badly hurt and had to be taken out of the arena in an ambulance. The rider after that was my older brother, who got his foot caught in the rope and was dragged around the arena for a while before they got him free. And then it was my turn. They always say bad luck comes in threes, and I seriously considered just giving up and not riding. I didn't want to end up like those guys! But I knew that if I didn't get on that bull, I'd never get on another one ever again. Once I let my fear win, it would just get bigger and bigger. So I gritted my teeth, faced my fear, and got on the bull. And in the end, I stayed on and came in second place! That day, I learned that the only way to handle my fear and discomfort was to address them directly. Delaying only gives them the chance to get bigger, scarier, and more uncomfortable.

Anytime we deceive, lie, or manipulate, all we're doing is delaying that moment of truth. Deception never solves the problem, and the truth will always come out. In the end, dishonesty is just us choosing not to get on the bull. And while that stops you from having to face your fear, it also prevents you from ever obtaining the prize. With each lie, the fear gets bigger and the discomfort more intense until deceit becomes the standard instead of the exception. An ethical leader knows that confronting difficult situations with honesty is the only way to effectively move past them.

I was able to learn a lot about how fear controls our decision-making from Tony Seidling. Tony is something of an expert on fear-based decision-making. He was a bull rider for nine years until a traumatic brain injury and broken neck made him think, "I have a wife and three kids. I should probably stop." After recovering from his injuries, he decided not to get back on a bull. Instead, he went skydiving. In fact, over the next two years, he went skydiving enough to become an instructor and has since taught more than 2,000 people how to skydive. Tony may be a bit of an adrenaline junkie, but it makes sense. Bull riding and skydiving have a lot of things in common. Both are completely unnatural. They're things that your instincts say you **should not do**! In his experience with thousands of different participants, Tony noticed that in the throes of the "fight or flight" response induced by both skydiving and bull riding, people responded in one of two ways. They either worried about being safe, or they worried about being successful.

The people who worry about being safe never move past their fear. They jump out of the plane and immediately start to worry about whether they're going to land safely instead of enjoying the experience, focusing on proper form, and keeping track of elevation. Their minds are consumed with getting back to safety. These people are so worried about landing that they are more likely to make mistakes when it comes to essentials like opening their parachute at the right time. Instead of riding it out and getting off safely, they worry about getting off the bull **right now** regardless of the consequences.

On the other hand, some people move past their first fear response. Instead of worrying about getting back on the ground, they focus on enjoying the experience and doing what needs to be done to reach their goal.

Tony refers to that how-do-I-get-to-safety mindset as "freefall thinking." It's the moment where you hit freefall and your brain says, "NOPE!" The *only* thing your mind and body want is for your current experience to be replaced with something comforting and safe.

Honesty is just like bull riding and skydiving. When you get confronted with an uncomfortable situation or conversation, your fear response tells you to take the shortest route to safety and comfort. Unfortunately, that route is usually through deception. Deception lets you avoid responsibility, discomfort, and vulnerability—at least in the short term. But that's freefall thinking. Instead, you need to think about what will make you successful—not what will make you safe and comfortable. And what will make you successful? Confronting the truth and being honest.

An Honest Bull

You may sometimes hear announcers or cowboys refer to a bull as honest. Something like, "That's a real honest bull. He's just out there doing his job." An "honest" bull stands nice in the chute, bucks his heart out, and then goes on his way.

Other bulls are less honest. They'll try to smash you against the chute before the ride starts and go out of their way to beat you to a pulp once you hit the ground. These bulls might be described as "playing dirty."

HONESTY REQUIRES DISCRETION

Many books, movies, and TV shows have explored how a world without dishonesty would look. But these "honest worlds" often miss two crucial elements: compassion and discretion. You'll usually see characters saying everything that comes to their minds as if everything they think is perfectly honest. For example, in the 1997 film "Liar, Liar," the main character is "cursed" to be completely honest for a day. When he enters his office, an overweight coworker asks, "What's up, Fletcher?" He instantly responds, "Your cholesterol, fatty!" before looking appalled that those words came out of his mouth. Regardless of how you define it, this isn't honesty. Honesty doesn't require you to say every single thought that enters your mind. There are plenty of things that are true that don't necessarily need to be said, and plenty of thoughts that cross our minds that aren't necessarily "true."

Honesty is more than just saying things that are true. Effective honesty requires us to discern what true things *need* to be said. Otherwise, we would walk around like dysfunctional robots constantly spouting things like "That's a cloud," "My left big toe is mildly uncomfortable," "I ate some toast today," "Your hair is longer than mine," and nothing productive would ever get done. The things you say should be honest, but not every honest thing needs to be said. There's a reason why the long-beloved Code of the West includes the item, "Talk less and say more."

Honesty—especially scary, uncomfortable honesty—needs to provide some sort of benefit to the situation. Lying is never* the answer, but sometimes diplomatic silence is better than saying every "true" thing that comes to mind.

Talk less. Say more.

HONESTY REQUIRES COMPASSION

When determining what honesty is helpful and what honesty isn't, compassion is absolutely necessary. Without compassion, it's far too easy to be cruel, demeaning, and rude under the guise of "telling it like it is." The importance of compassion in honest communication isn't a new idea. Kim Scott explored

---

*There are a few very rare exceptions, when somebody's life or personal safety are on the line. But these are exceptions that most of us will never face.

the topic thoroughly in her book, "Radical Candor," where being directly honest without caring personally is referred to as "Obnoxious Aggression." Bruce Kasanoff has famously said, "Honesty without compassion is cruelty." I love the phrasing of that quote. It isn't, "Honesty without compassion is ineffective" or "Honesty without compassion isn't ideal." Those would imply that compassion is simply a tool to make honesty more useful. But it isn't. It's a requirement. **Honesty without compassion isn't honesty at all.** It's just cruelty.

PRACTICING HONESTY

You may think that developing honesty would be as simple as "just stop lying." But unfortunately, there are a lot of deeply ingrained habits in most people that prevent honesty, such as justification, telling partial truths, and obscuring the truth. You'll have to identify these habits and recondition yourself so that honesty becomes your default behavior. Here are some ideas on how to start.

- At the end of each day, write down any instances of dishonesty and deception that you noticed throughout the day. Ask yourself what fear or discomfort you were trying to avoid. Brainstorm how honesty could have helped the situation.

- When you notice yourself bending the truth, quickly correct it. Often, when we find ourselves tending towards dishonesty, many of us double down on our lies. Instead, a simple, "Sorry, I was wrong" followed by the full truth can usually fix the situation with minimal awkwardness—and certainly much less than when the truth comes out later.

IMPLEMENTATION INTENTIONS

- When someone asks me for feedback, I will make sure to give them sincere and honest feedback in a compassionate way.

- _____
  _____

- _____
  _____

CHAPTER EIGHT

AUTHENTICITY

"AUTHENTICITY IS MORE THAN SPEAKING. AUTHENTICITY IS ALSO ABOUT DOING. EVERY DECISION WE MAKE SAYS SOMETHING ABOUT WHO WE ARE."

SIMON SINEK

Authenticity can mean many things, depending on who you ask. For the purposes of bull rider leadership, we're going to define authenticity as a type of integrity. Namely, authenticity is consistency between your beliefs, words, and actions.

Since I try to practice the determined optimism of a bull rider leader, I make an effort to focus on the positive instead of the negative. But sometimes, it is easier to understand the value of authenticity by looking at examples of *inauthentic* leaders.

GET ON THE BULL

Unfortunately, some of these examples may be all too familiar to you:

- A manager tells their team that they should be innovative and take risks, then reprimands or punishes them if their risks don't pay off. While their words say, "We want to foster innovation," their actions say, "Don't take risks."

- When recruiting, a company advertises the importance of work-life balance, saying that family is more important than work and there is unlimited approved time off. Then leaders assign heavy workloads with strict deadlines, message employees outside of work hours, and subtly guilt employees for taking needed time off.

- A supervisor is very strict about enforcing a policy that requires all employees to clock out for lunches and breaks. But that same supervisor rarely clocks out themselves.

If you've ever experienced managerial hypocrisy like this, I'm sorry. You probably know firsthand just how much behavior like this destroys trust, decreases job satisfaction, and absolutely devastates employee retention rates. It makes just about everything worse.

Authenticity helps us avoid these mistakes by developing consistency between what we say and what we do. If I say,

"I want you to take care of yourself," then I need to support you in taking a day off work if you're experiencing burnout. Not with a doctor's note, not with authorization from your therapist. Just letting you take care of yourself because I said I would. If I as a leader implement a rule or policy, I need to follow that rule or policy—even when it's inconvenient. *Especially* when it's inconvenient. I should feel the impact of my own decisions.

Trust blossoms when our actions and words are consistent with each other. But the true power of authenticity is unlocked when we also align our actions and our words with our beliefs.

Beliefs act as the foundation, the compass, if you will, of an authentic individual. Company values and visions are established to leverage the power of this principle. They provide a firm, defined belief that *should* dictate how employees behave. Unfortunately, how we *should* behave and how we *do* behave often differ. Too often, we have strong values that we firmly believe in and abide by—until it's too inconvenient. Or until those values cost us revenue, employees, or opportunities. And then those beliefs get put on the backburner.

An authentic leader will design systems, messaging, incentives, and everything else around their values. The single most common company value is "Teamwork." For that belief to be authentic and consistent, a leader should ensure that employees can communicate and collaborate easily, that they know and understand each other's strengths, and that they are rewarded for seeking help. If you list "Teamwork" as a guiding value and then incentivize individual performance and turn every activity into a competition, your value loses authenticity.

The level of alignment in your beliefs, words, and actions trickles down to those you lead, for better or worse. If the leadership is inauthentic, the employees will need to quickly learn to adapt to the unpredictable whims of the leader. And that's when compartmentalization starts to rear its ugly head.

THE DANGERS OF COMPARTMENTALIZATION

The definition of compartmentalization varies, but in psychology, it refers to a natural defense mechanism where we separate conflicting thoughts or feelings into different parts of our mind. In work environments, compartmentalization occurs when what we feel like we need to do conflicts with what we believe is right. For example, if a salesperson sincerely believes in being honest, but their work environment allows or even encourages stretching the truth or withholding important facts to make a sale, they may find themselves compartmentalizing. They'll extol the virtues of honesty at home and in their private lives while compromising their standards at work under the justification of "Just doing my job."

The phrases "I'm just doing my job," "It's nothing personal," and "It's just business" are responsible for some of the greatest scandals and atrocities across the world. And while "Just doing their job" could assuredly be applied to German soldiers during World War II, the dangers of these phrases can also be found in examples closer to home.

I knew a man named Brad who went into business with a close friend of his. And just from that first sentence, you can probably guess how this ends. Because they were such good friends and trusted each other so much, their contracts were vague. They mostly just had a general agreement to treat each other well and split everything 50/50. For a few years, the business and partnership worked out great! But after a sudden and devastating string of bad luck, Brad's partner found himself in a difficult financial position and needed to sell his share of the company. Brad offered to buy him out, but because they had never officially settled on the valuation terms and because his partner was desperate, Brad found himself in a very powerful position. Completely legally and fairly according to contract law, he had the opportunity to acquire the other half of the business for way less than the share was truly worth. Brad knew that, morally, this behavior was questionable. But in the heat of the moment and with the opportunity of a lifetime within his grasp, he found it easy to compartmentalize. In the final conversation with his partner, where he was either faced with accepting Brad's offer or taking it to court, Brad assured him, "This has nothing to do with our friendship. It's just business."

Unsurprisingly, that close personal friendship withered. Because while Brad had compartmentalized his feelings, his partner hadn't—and couldn't. Someone he trusted had hurt him in his time of need, and that doesn't just go away because they say, "It isn't personal."

Compartmentalization, hypocrisy, and inconsistency are just some of the ways that we can be inauthentic. And even the few examples we've covered show how detrimental a lack of authenticity can be. So let's take a break from the negative examples and focus a bit more on the positive side of what genuine authenticity looks like and the benefits it can have.

I had the chance to interview a man who exemplified authentic consistency. One of his core beliefs was that he should be honest in all his dealings with those around him. He felt that if he gave his word, whether on a contract or in person, he needed to stand by that commitment. And living that way had worked out very well for him! He was a millionaire before he turned 30, owned a thriving and expanding business, was an influential member of the community, and had a blossoming young family. And things just kept looking better. An opportunity presented itself to acquire one of his largest competitors, and in a separate stroke of good fortune, he got a steal of a deal on a prime piece of land for subdivision and development. Over the next few years, he was projected to make millions.

Then the 2008 financial crisis hit him like a bus. Just after acquiring his competitor, the entire industry tanked, making it nearly impossible to keep up with the acquisition debt he had incurred. At the same time, a windmill construction project was announced right next to his subdivided land. That announcement brought the property's appraised value from $1.9 million to $850,000, effectively costing him $1.1 million overnight. In just a few weeks, his rapidly growing wealth had vanished, and he was left with more than $1.5 million of debt. He had listened to his accountants and his advisors. He hadn't taken any unreasonable risks, especially with the information he had at the time. But it had been the perfect storm of unforeseen circumstances, and it left him destitute.

Those same accountants and advisors now encouraged him to declare bankruptcy. This, they argued, was a textbook example of why bankruptcy exists. Nothing that had happened was his fault, and no one would fault him for simply walking away from it all. But this man disagreed. Because he believed strongly in supporting local businesses, he had taken out loans from smaller, local banks–banks who would be dealt a severe blow if he defaulted on those loans. He had given them his word that he would pay back those loans. He had made promises to people, and he intended to keep those promises.

He worked hard, he sold his assets, and over the course of nearly 15 years, he paid off the entire debt.

Regardless of whether you think this man is a fool or a hero, he is authentic. He doesn't compartmentalize. He believes in standing by his word. What he says and what he does are in harmony with that belief. And when you talk to him, you can *feel* it. Even if you disagree with him, you can't help but respect his authenticity.

THE BENEFITS OF AUTHENTICITY

Some of the most significant benefits of authenticity will be seen in your personal life as well as your work environment. Authenticity has been linked to increased confidence, self-esteem, and happiness. These positive changes cascade into a variety of interpersonal benefits like stronger relationships.

Authenticity has also been shown to increase loyalty, engagement, and job satisfaction in the workplace. Part of this increase can be attributed to our inherent ability to sense when someone or something feels "off." When someone isn't acting "themselves," we can usually tell, even if we can't quite put our finger on what it is. Authenticity removes that sense of "off-ness" and eliminates a lot of subtle workplace tension. When everyone feels comfortable being themselves, they form stronger bonds, work more cohesively as a team, and are even shown to behave more ethically. The list goes on and on, with other benefits rippling out from increased trust and confidence due to authenticity.

IMPERFECTION IS AUTHENTIC

While the goal is for our beliefs, words, and actions to be perfectly in line, realistically, that probably isn't going to happen. Remember, we *all* fall off the bull. Some would have you believe that falling short of your ideals makes you a hypocrite. For example, the previous section addresses the fact that honesty is a crucial value to practice. You may tell your team that you value honesty, that you will be honest with them, and that you want them to be honest with you. But you'll probably still have moments of dishonesty. It's unfortunate but realistic.

Falling short of your own professed ideals isn't hypocrisy—it's humanity. Your authenticity will largely be determined by how you handle those imperfect moments. The key is to humbly take responsibility for your mistakes and apologize to those you harmed. But even more importantly, you need to offer understanding and grace to those who also fall short. People don't resent leaders who make mistakes. They resent leaders who hide their mistakes, while punishing others who behave in a similar way.

CHANGE IS AUTHENTIC

Sometimes our beliefs, words, and actions don't line up because something has changed. There are those who will tell you that if you espouse a particular belief and then say something contradictory, you must be an inauthentic, hypocritical, noncommittal, gutless flip-flopper. While inconsistency in your beliefs and what you say can be problematic, sometimes it just means that you've changed, grown, or matured. Or perhaps you've gathered new information and seen a different perspective, which created a change of opinion.

Whether it's opinions, beliefs, behaviors, or how we speak, change is a normal—and hopefully positive—part of life. Authenticity doesn't mean staying exactly the same forever. It's just being genuine about who you are, growth and all.

FALLING SHORT OF YOUR OWN PROFESSED IDEALS ISN'T HYPOCRISY—IT'S HUMANITY.

PRACTICING AUTHENTICITY

Because authenticity requires your beliefs, actions, and behaviors to align, it's important to be *aware* of your beliefs, thoughts, and actions. Here are some tips for discovering and then aligning these important elements of your character:

- Brainstorm your beliefs. This doesn't mean writing down a bunch of religious doctrines. It's about making sure you can verbalize what's important to *you*. You may want to sort these beliefs in order of priority. This helps you see if what you *say* is "most important" aligns with how you spend your time.

- Be deliberate. This is in the same vein as being honest and following the cowboy code of "Talk less, say more." Slow down and make sure the things you say and do align with your beliefs. Words and decisions made in the heat of the moment are less likely to be authentic to your values.

- Get help. Someone who knows you well, like a spouse or close friend, can let you know when you're contradictory, inconsistent, or inauthentic. If you ask someone to help you identify your inauthentic moments, *listen to them!* Even if it's hard.

IMPLEMENTATION INTENTION

- While eating lunch each day, I will examine the biggest decision I made that morning to determine whether it is consistent with my beliefs and words.

- _____
  _____

- _____
  _____

CHAPTER NINE

GRIT

"IN EVERY TRIUMPH THERE'S A LOT OF TRY."

FRANK TYGER

B elieve it or not, grit isn't just a slang term to refer to people who don't give up. It's actually an official term used in the study of human psychology. The American Psychological Association defines grit as:

> "A personality trait characterized by perseverance and passion for achieving long-term goals. Grit entails working strenuously to overcome challenges and maintaining effort and interest over time despite failures, adversities, and plateaus in progress. Recent studies suggest this trait may be more relevant than intelligence in determining a person's high achievement. For example, grit may be particularly important to accomplishing an

especially complex task when there is a strong temptation to give up altogether."

Grit, often just called "try" in the rodeo world, is the behavioral equivalent of determined optimism. It's taking that attitude and putting it into practice. Successful leaders **need** to be able to handle setbacks, challenges, and failures without giving up. And I'm not messing around with the emphasis on the word "need" there. To succeed long-term, grit is absolutely required. Angela Duckworth, the psychologist who pretty much invented the concept of grit as we know it, found in her studies that grit is a better indicator of success than talent, experience, intelligence, or anything else.

People with grit are successful. They may not be successful immediately, but they'll always succeed simply because **they do not stop trying.** When other people have long given up, gritty people are still doing what it takes to reach their goals, regardless of the challenges they face.

Bull riders take grit to an extreme (and occasionally hazardous) level. At the 2021 PBR World Championships, rookie bull rider Eli Vastbinder broke several ribs and separated his shoulder during his third-round ride. He got a re-ride option, took it despite his injuries, and ended up scoring 90 while riding with freshly broken ribs. This put him solidly in the running for World Champion. But there were still two more rides between him and any kind of victory. He got on anyway, scoring another 90 point ride followed by an amazing 92.75

point ride. After each round, Eli crawled to safety, barely able to breathe while medical staff looked him over to **make sure none of his already broken ribs had punctured a lung.**

Eli placed fifth in the World Finals and earned the "Rookie of the Year" PBR title for his effort. When everyone started telling him how tough he was, he didn't seem to think it was all that special. This was his response:

> "It doesn't hurt too bad before I get on and in the bucking chutes. It is just after. It is breathtaking for quite a while. I don't feel it when I ride. It is just when I hit the ground and I feel it. There is not much toughness other than dealing with it afterwards for the next hour or so, just until you get the breath back and things ease up a bit.
>
> "I rodeoed for years. I ride bulls. It is no different if it was anybody else. They all would have done the same thing I was doing right now."

For Eli, this is just what you do. You keep going, keep working, and do your best, regardless of your discomfort. You don't quit.

Now, grit doesn't mean completely disregarding your physical and mental well-being. If the medical staff had told Eli he couldn't ride, he wouldn't have ridden, end of story. He made sure he had medical clearance and his wife's support. Then he did what he had to do and got the treatment he could along the way.

While Eli's story is impressive, it isn't all that uncommon in the rodeo world. Every bull rider I've talked to (and that's quite a few) has had a story to share of pushing through injuries or discouragement. It's just part of the sport.

And those experiences aren't just confined to the world of bull riding. Stephen King, Dr. Suess, and J.K. Rowling were all rejected by publishers at least a dozen times. James Dyson made 5,126 failed prototypes before creating the vacuum cleaner that made him a multi-billionaire. Michael Jordan was cut from his high school basketball team. And of course, there's the famous Thomas Edison quote, "I have not failed—I've successfully found 10,000 ways that will not work."

Name any "overnight success," and they likely had years and years of failure and struggle before finally making it big. Nobody changes the world on their first try. It takes time, effort, and a lot of failures along the way.

GRIT REQUIRES INNOVATION

Success is a journey, and grit is what keeps us moving forward on that journey. But grit isn't just stubbornly bashing your head against a wall until you break through it. Insanity is famously described as doing the same thing repeatedly while expecting a different result. Gritty people do more than just keep trying. They try *differently* when things don't work. They innovate, experiment, and explore. A gritty leader is willing to take risks, because they aren't afraid of failing. Instead of bringing them down, they know that any failures will just propel them to future success.

A STORY BY STEVE COOPER

I once drew a bull that was a little famous in the pro rodeo circuit at the time. *Nobody* had successfully ridden this guy. But he had a bit of a pattern. Usually, when he left the chute, he would pull into a hard left turn that would send people flying. So one of my buddies suggested I put my hand lower on the left side of the bull rope to give me more control during a left spin. I was a little hesitant. "What if he turns right instead?" I asked. "I'll get thrown right away."

He replied saying, "Everyone else has been thrown anyway. May as well give it a try."

So I did. I took the risk, lowered my hand, the bull did his usual left spin—and he threw me off anyway. I stayed on for a few seconds, but I didn't make the buzzer. It was worth a shot, though!

91

DON'T CONFUSE GRIT WITH OBSESSION

I want to be extremely careful about how I address this, because swinging too far in either direction is problematic. Grit is pursuing your goals with passion and perseverance. But it's okay for your goals and priorities to change. You may remember Seth Glause's story from earlier, where he wanted to be the World Champion but kept hurting his shoulder. Some might say that Seth didn't show enough grit because he quit. Those people would be wrong. Seth decided that his health and his family were more important than becoming World Champion, so he decided to stop riding and become a coach instead. His goal changed, but he still pursues the new goal of being an excellent coach, husband, and father with as much passion and perseverance as the old goal. Let me reiterate: Priorities and circumstances change throughout life. Sometimes we "quit" pursuing one goal to achieve another, more important one. That isn't failing—it's prioritizing.

BALANCE, NOT BURNOUT

In a world filled with "hustle culture," side gigs, and burnout, it's important to recognize that grit is **not** working yourself to death at the expense of everything else. The reasons we work are to provide for ourselves and our loved ones, find fulfillment, make a positive impact in the world, and even for fun and enjoyment. Grit isn't about doing more or harder work just for the sake of it. It's about pursuing your personal and professional goals with passion and dedication. It's refusing to quit just because things get hard. It's seeing commitments through to completion. It's doing your best, even when you have every reason not to.

To effectively utilize grit, you must consider the long-term. Achieving your goals can often take months, years, or decades. To pursue them with dedication, you have to *still* be sane enough to pursue them at all! That's why grit is a principle of balance. As cliché as it is, the saying, "Life is a marathon, not a sprint," definitely applies here. If you were to wake up one day and say, "I'm going to run a marathon," and then proceed to jump out of bed, run out your door at top speed, and do your best to maintain that speed for 26.2 miles, no amount of determination would stop you from collapsing. If you repeat that process every day for months, you may start seeing progress, or more likely, you may end up in the hospital. That isn't grit. It's reckless and unproductive.

Let's imagine a different scenario. You wake up one day and say, "I'm going to run a marathon." Then you jump out of bed and do some research on marathons. You learn about training programs and proper nutrition. Then you go for a jog. You may train on your own for a while, or you may eventually talk to a personal trainer that can help guide you on your journey. You learn to make sure you're hydrated for long runs. You get good equipment to avoid chafing, blisters, and other discomforts. It may take some time, but with that trajectory, you will end up successfully running a marathon. Keeping that trajectory going takes preparation, patience, and discipline; in short, it takes **grit**.

Even as I write this, I can hear the objections. "But Dallin, wasn't it reckless for Eli Vastbinder to ride those bulls injured? He wouldn't have reached his goal if he'd punctured a lung and died! Why does that count as grit?" And that's a good objection. But there's an important difference between Eli's behavior and reckless burnout behavior. The difference is that Eli had been training for the 2021 World Finals for 27 years. Ever since he first tried to ride a sheep at three years old, Eli had been preparing, learning, and training his mind and body to ride bulls. He had doctors on hand and medical clearance to continue as well as approval from his wife.

If you train for 27 years to run a marathon and sprain your ankle 100 feet from the end, and then you get a doctor's clearance to limp to the finish line, that doesn't sound reckless to me.

That sounds like grit.

PRACTICING GRIT

Since grit is a mindset put into action, you can develop it by improving the mindset. In addition to the items listed below, use the action items under "Determined Optimism" to help you develop grit.

- Read/Listen to stories about grit. Part of the reason motivational speakers exist is because they work. When people hear stories about success and determination, they gain a desire to succeed themselves and to work harder to do so.

- Write down your goals and put them somewhere visible. Our dedication to a goal increases when it's written down and increases even more when it is somewhere we see often.

- Share your successes. While keeping humility in mind, celebrate victories with those close to you, even if they are just small victories along the way. Taking note of progress is important to help keep you from getting discouraged.

IMPLEMENTATION INTENTION

- If I feel discouraged about a goal or project, I will listen to a motivational podcast.

- _____
_____

- _____
_____

CHAPTER TEN

SERVICE

> **"RULE WITH THE HEART OF A SERVANT.**
> **SERVE WITH THE HEART OF A KING."**
>
> **BILL JOHNSON**

When you're in the chute getting on a bull, you need somebody to tighten your bull rope before you can ride. In high school and college rodeos, you have a friend or competitor help you out and tighten the rope. In larger, more competitive rodeos, you probably still have a friend or competitor tighten the bull rope. At the National Finals Rodeo, with piles of money on the line and more than a million people watching, you *still* have a friend or competitor come help you tighten the bull rope.

Bull riding is a competitive sport, but it's also one of the most service-driven communities you'll ever find. While most professional athletes have crews of attendants and assistants taking care of every detail behind the scenes, bull riders instead choose to help the very people they're competing against. I've never talked to a bull rider who hasn't at some point hitched a ride with a competitor to get to the next rodeo or who hasn't helped another rider in a time of need.

Remember Eli Vastbinder? The guy who rode three bulls back-to-back with broken ribs? When he got back to his hotel, he couldn't even bend over enough to take off his socks. So he called his friend and fellow rider, Boudreaux Campbell, who came over and helped him get out of his socks. And if leaving your comfy hotel room to go help your buddy out of his nasty, sweaty socks isn't service, I don't know what is.

Want to know what's even better? The only reason Eli was in the position to even ride at the World Finals is because 11 years earlier, the previous World Champion, J.B. Mauney, paid for Eli's plane ticket to get to his first event. Acts of service compound as each person pays it forward and helps those around them.

"Servant leadership" has been something of a buzzword since 1970, with a primary focus on inverting the classic leadership hierarchy to emphasize that the more people you lead, the more people you should be serving.

A LEADER WHO CARES ENOUGH TO ASK, TO LEARN, TO TRY AND UNDERSTAND IS A LEADER WHO WILL NOT ONLY BE MORE EFFECTIVE BUT WILL EARN THE LOYALTY OF THOSE THEY LEAD.

Like many leadership styles, servant leadership has pros and cons. But regardless of your preferred leadership style, service is absolutely crucial to your success. Service helps eliminate selfishness and turns competitive environments into collaborative ones. In other words, instead of pitting ourselves against each other, we pull together as a team to pit ourselves against a problem. When team members feel the need to jockey for power or make plans to get ahead, everybody becomes less effective. A strong team needs to be united in solving problems and accomplishing goals, not claiming credit or "winning" against their teammates.

When asked about the constant acts of service seen amongst riders, Seth Glause, retired bull rider and current rodeo coach, said:

"I never saw the other riders as competitors. I just saw them as friends. And we needed to be there to help our friends and help our community. I see it with the students I teach now. They're always helping each other, and they truly love to see each other succeed. It's great to see the next generation really caring about each other."

This behavior is directly linked with one of the bull rider attitudes we discussed earlier: perspective. One study done by the National Academy of Sciences indicated that service can increase empathy and understanding. Service puts human relationships at the forefront and eliminates tensions between different groups. It shifts our perspectives, making us think about people **as people.** The more you serve, the more you understand the individuals you serve. The more you understand those individuals, the more invested you'll be in them and their happiness. When you're a leader, service isn't just about helping the people you already care about. Service is *the way you learn to care.*

And I mean that very literally. Organizational psychologist Benjamin Hardy has taught how investing yourself in something changes how you feel about it. He said:

> "You love what you invest yourself in. You love who you invest yourself in. Your relationships become meaningful as they benefit others. Your skills become meaningful as they serve and benefit others. No investment, no attachment."

This principle can apply to anyone and anything. If you invest yourself in your work, you'll love your work. If you volunteer at an animal shelter, you'll love the animals. And if you serve those you lead, you'll come to understand and care about them not just as employees or subordinates but as *people.*

And then a magical thing happens. Because reciprocity is a fundamental principle of human nature, those same individuals will stop seeing you as a boss or manager. Instead, they'll see you as a person. And while they may serve you in return, it's more likely that they'll do something even better. They will start to serve each other, and they'll serve those *they* lead.

Deep in our hearts and brains, humans want to help and serve each other. But prolonged exposure to certain cultures and environments can start to numb that instinct. Things like a fear of awkwardness (which we all share) can transform even the smallest actions into moments of paralyzing indecision. Perhaps the best example of this is the simplest and most innocent act of service of all time: holding the door for someone.

It's so simple. It shouldn't be a big deal. But depending on the context and your service culture, it's easy to start second-guessing everything! Is the person far enough away that it's going to feel weird? Will they do that awkward half-jog so they don't inconvenience me? There are quite a few people behind them. Do I hold the door for all of them? When do I stop? If I'm a man and the other person is a woman, am I accidentally making some kind of statement? Am I crossing a line? Do I stand behind the door and go in after them or stand half in the doorway and stretch my arm out to keep it open and let them catch it? Is that too halfhearted of an effort? You freeze in your moment of indecision before giving up and leaving the door to close in their face.

And that's a simple example! Many people don't serve others because they are afraid of offending them, crossing some "social acceptability" line, or just coming off as weird. But when people see a leader demonstrate a culture of service by sincerely seeking to help those around them, it can remove the social barriers and free others to serve as well.

SINCERE SERVICE BUILDS LOYALTY

In January 2020, I sold my marketing agency and took a management contract with the new company as part of the transition. By March 2020, the COVID-19 pandemic had shut down practically everything, and in May 2020, my wife and I had our first child. It was an eventful few months, to say the least. And to top it all off, there were several terrifying complications during labor for my wife. At the end of the day, both she and the baby were fine. She was released from the hospital with our brand-new, squeaky, helpless little bundle of humanity. Normally, we would have had lots of helpful volunteers from around our neighborhood and church community to aid us in the struggles of new parenthood. However, the pandemic was still in its early stages, and everyone was very cautious about visiting the home of a newborn. And we didn't want to put our little guy at risk, either! So we found ourselves isolated, exhausted, and confused, trying to figure out how to be new parents in the middle of a global pandemic.

One day we received a message from our new employer asking what day and time would be most helpful for dinner to show up. They sent us a delicious meal, which we devoured with as much enthusiasm as our sleep-deprived brains and bodies would allow. It was a small thing, but it meant so much in a time when we felt so alone. By this time, we had only been a part of this company for four months, and only two of those months had been pre-COVID. In the midst of dealing with the pandemic, and *on top of* handling all the intricacy of a merger, this small act of service earned our loyalty and made us feel even better about the deal we'd made four months earlier. And, quite simply, it made that one day a little bit easier, which at that point in our lives, made us more grateful than words can say.

Serving others builds their trust and loyalty, but only when that service is sincere. Service that comes with strings attached, such as vendors wining and dining big clients, does work. But at that point, it stops being service. It becomes a marketing tactic and a subtle transactional dance. And while it may be effective, it isn't going to transform relationships, inspire trust, and build loyalty in the same way that sincere service does.

Practicing Service:

- Actively look for opportunities to serve. Don't wait for people to come to you or say, "Let me know if you need anything." Be proactive in finding ways to help.

- Ask the right questions. When seeking to serve, ask specific questions, not just the vague but well-meaning platitudes that most people habitually use. Consider the difference in the following questions/statements.

Ineffective	Effective
Is there anything I can do to help?	What would make your job easier?
Let me know if you need anything.	Would it help if I (specify a helpful action)?
Do you need help?	Can I help?

- Listen. You may be starting to notice that you can improve a lot of leadership behaviors by listening. It really is just that important.

- Allow others to serve you. You have to take the lead in creating a culture of service, not just in serving others, but in allowing them to serve you.

IMPLEMENTATION INTENTION

- When someone asks if they can help me, I will say yes.

- _____
  _____

- _____
  _____

CONCLUSION

At the beginning of this book, we talked about how people are inspired when others do incredible things. Stories and principles of success motivate us. Hopefully, reading this book has motivated you to be a better leader. That's great! But motivation often forms a problematic cycle. First, you get inspired to change, so you make broad, drastic, wildly ambitious goals. Achieving those goals quickly becomes exhausting and leads to burnout, which leads to all the progress being lost until you read this book (or a similar one) again and get excited to once again try and do better! Like a New Year's diet or gym attendance resolution, this cycle is based on good intentions but can often do more harm than good.

Instead, we should take Seth Glause's advice from earlier and work on one thing at a time. Don't put this book down and say, "I'm going to be perfectly honest and grateful for everyone while serving my entire community with humble, determined optimism." Not only is that so jam-packed full of buzzwords that it hurt me a little to write it, but it's also vague and unrealistic. All of the attitudes and behaviors discussed in this book are good. But you're probably already better at some than others. Choose one that feels like it would truly benefit your life and situation right now, set a specific and achievable goal, and then pursue that goal. When you feel like you've turned the goal into a habit, revisit this book and choose another. Then another. And another. Consistent, disciplined progress that builds over time is more effective than short bursts of motivation.

THE IMPORTANCE OF NUANCE

We've addressed this multiple times at this point, but it's worth repeating: People are complicated. Books, videos, inspiring quotes, and motivational speakers tend to paint pictures of humanity with broad strokes so they can connect with a large audience. But we have only a limited time with a whole lot of people, which often means we can't tailor our message to fit everyone's exact situation. I've tried to make sure the advice and principles found in this book are scientifically sound and effective for most people. But every recommendation still requires some individual adaptation on occasion. For example, many would agree that making eye contact with someone when speaking to them is good for building trust and rapport. But if you're speaking to a neurodivergent individual, that same level of eye contact can be very uncomfortable for them. In that situation, you'd need to adapt for you both to communicate effectively.

The principles in this book are the same way. Developing these attitudes and behaviors **will make you a better leader**. But there will always be situations that call for nuance. A compassionate act of service in one company might be considered an inappropriate breach of conduct in another. An honest, authentic, and humble request for help from a leader can empower a team and build trust by showing that the leader trusts them and their expertise. That exact same request could have the opposite effect if voiced in a time of crisis when that same team is looking for someone to be strong and in control.

Just like every bull and every ride will be a little different, there is no "one size fits all" solution to effectively leading. You'll need to make adjustments to make these principles work their best for you. And there's only one way to get there.

GET ON THE BULL

One year at the Wyoming State Fair, my dad and I found a group of young men staring down a mechanical bull. Of course, they were doing what most teenage boys would do in that situation:

bragging and making bets. These were all farm and ranch kids who considered themselves pretty tough, so they thought they would show how cool they were and win the bet by staying on the longest. Standard bull riding rules applied: Keep your free hand in the air and don't let it touch the bull. And most of them put in a decent showing. They each stayed on for 10-20 seconds as the operator slowly ramped up the difficulty. I joined in and did a decent (but by no means "bet-winning") job myself. A couple of the kids knew that my dad had been a bull rider in his youth. They started goading him to take a ride and show them how it's done. There were more than a few "old man" jokes thrown in since my Dad was into his 50s and hadn't ridden a bull in decades. After some hemming and hawing, he finally relented, paid the fee, and got up on the bull. The operator started slowly, but Dad looked him in the eyes and gave the bull a hard spur to make it clear he didn't want to be coddled. By 30 seconds or so, the operator was giving it everything he had, and Dad remained completely unfazed. Around a minute in, the operator gave up and stopped the bull. Everyone watching (myself included) was absolutely stunned. The boys were humbled, and I was filled with a shocked pride. Who knew my dad was such a stud?

As we walked away, Dad told me that he'd had a lot of fun, but the mechanical bull just couldn't compare to the real thing. That had been clear to anybody watching. But a mechanical bull is still the closest substitute we have if you want to practice riding a bull without actually getting on one. So if you've ridden a mechanical bull and still want to improve, what do you do? Well, there's really only one option.

Get on the real bull.

Sometimes, there's just no substitute for actual experience. Training, workshops, podcasts, and books like this one all have a valuable place in teaching us lessons and providing new insights. But they won't *make* you a great leader. There comes a time where you have to put down the book and start practicing the principles in the high-risk environment that is the real world. You'll mess up. You'll make mistakes that leave you winded in the dirt of the arena of life. But that's okay. Own those mistakes. Learn from them. It's the only way you'll ever become the life-changing leader that you're capable of becoming. It's time to put down the book and get on the bull.

ACKNOWLEDGMENTS

It takes so many people to make a book happen. And this one never would have happened without the support of my wonderful wife, Caitee. Like many people, I kicked around the idea of writing a book for years, but it was her encouragement that finally helped me get started. She spent hours talking through the base concepts and providing insight from her background in psychology, as well as acting as the first-round editor. Literally every single line of this book has been affected by Caitee's input. It wouldn't have happened without her.

Of course, it also wouldn't have happened without my dad, Steve Cooper. He's the inspiration for the entire book, and his stories and lessons not only shaped the principles in the book, they shaped my life. Dad, thank you for sharing your stories. I hope they change other people's lives the same way they changed mine.

Taking a book from a fun idea to an actual reality is daunting. Wilene Dunn, my speaking agent and advisor, was invaluable at guiding me through the process and keeping everything moving on a steady timeline. I'm easily frozen by analysis paralysis, but Wilene was always able to snap me out of it and help move things forward. A huge thank you to my editor, Shannon Dunn, for her attention to detail and putting up with my strong opinions about grammar as a social convention.

Last, but certainly not least, this book wouldn't have been possible without all the other cowboys I interviewed. In particular thank you to Seth Glause and Tony Seidling, for your time, insights, and stories.

ABOUT THE AUTHOR

Dallin is a speaker and consultant on ethics and leadership. He founded a digital marketing agency, a pet food company, and lived as a shepherd. He lives with his wife and two sons in Wyoming, but is often found on LinkedIn or dallincooper.com.

JOURNAL

JOURNAL

CPSIA information can be obtained
at www.ICGtesting.com
Printed in the USA
BVHW090507060722
641300BV00011B/1252